The Complete Experience

the secrets of online reviews
that drive customer loyalty

Tony Bodoh and Kayla Barrett

Copyright © 2017 Tony Bodoh and Kayla Barrett

All rights reserved.

ISBN: 978-0-9857142-2-2

ENDORSEMENTS

"Great and quick read. Unique insights into the world of online reviews backed up with relatable real world examples. This book not only applies to people in customer experience, but support, product and brand."

Chris Jones
Speaker, Customer Experience Expert and Chief
Customer Officer at Beartooth

"Tony Bodoh and Kayla Barrett have discovered, developed and presented a simple and unique insight into online customer reviews that unpacks what each and every business must know yet oftentimes does not see even when it is right in front of them. More importantly, they layout highly successful strategies, action steps and leadership insights to keep any business agile and responsive to keep customers coming back."

David Norris
Executive Coach and Former Chief Operating
Officer of Happy State Bank

"As an executive from a highly respected cultural attraction, I have become keenly aware of how online reviews can both positively and negatively impact guest expectations. However, with guest feedback coming from a variety of sources it often is difficult to identify core issues and provide proper strategies to ensure success in a competitive market.

Tony and Kayla's book, 'The Complete Experience: Unlocking the secrets of online reviews that drive customer loyalty' provided me with useful tools to better analyze online reviews. Specifically to not only better understand our key customer experience drivers but outlined a clear pathway to defining what we want as the ideal customer experience.

Additionally, I appreciated their insight into the importance of providing opportunities to get your engaged employees the highest visibility and interaction with your customers to produce the greatest results.

I am excited about the prospect of applying these principles and encourage an environment which embraces online feedback to help guide organizational decisions enabling us to remain a success story within our industry."

Dennis Schnurbusch II
Director of Visitor Services, Toledo Zoo
and Aquarium

THE COMPLETE EXPERIENCE

CONTENTS

INTRODUCTION

"Is there anyone so wise as to learn by the experience of others?"

Voltaire – Historian and Philosopher

"The only source of knowledge is experience."

Albert Einstein –Nobel Prize in Physics

Companies of every type include this goal as one of their top three: create higher revenues with lower operational costs. In other words, profit. However, in spite of that goal, three converging forces in the marketplace today are making it tough to achieve strong profits.

1. Your customers are demanding higher value for their money

The new normal of a tighter economy has created an unwillingness for customers to risk purchasing poor quality products or tolerating poor service experiences, even at reduced prices. They expect companies to not just chase the leaders in their industries, but to adopt or adapt best practices from other industries. They reason, "If Zappos can do it, why can't every call center?"

2. Your employees are being targeted

The war to acquire the greatest talent is intensifying and your best employees may be courted by other companies. Professionals are more actively exploring job opportunities than in previous years. According to Bersin by Deloitte, job seeker confidence and employee mobility is rising. 30% of the workforce is more actively reaching out to personal networks and are more often open to talking to a recruiter.

3. Strangers are influencing your customers' buying behaviors

There is an increase in the influence online reviews have on purchasing decisions in many industries. In a 2014 study by BrightLocal, 88% of consumers trust online reviews as much as personal recommendations. In addition, 80% of people changed their purchase decisions due to poor online reviews. The opportunity to review products and services extend from the traditional sectors of hotels and restaurants to professional sectors like dentists, doctors and lawyers. Most retail companies have product reviews on their websites. Amazon, Best Buy and Home Depot are just three examples.

Why this book matters now

Together, these three forces are creating unique challenges for businesses of every type. In the following pages we reveal a behind-the-scenes glimpse of the relationship between your online reviews and consumer behavior. The five secrets will change how you view your customer ratings and comments. But we don't stop there. These secrets also provide insight to solutions for your business. Are you are ready to achieve more 5-star ratings? Then read on.

PRACTICAL INSIGHTS

SECRET #1

Online reviews impact virtually every business today

"It's kind of astonishing that people trust strangers because of words they write on computer screens."

Howard Rheingold – Author and Lecturer

"If two people believe in the same story, they might be thousands of miles apart and total strangers, but they still have a sense they can trust each other."

James Altucher – Entrepreneur, Author

The surge in online influence demonstrates the brutal fact that customer service is no longer good enough. Loyalty AND satisfaction are the name of the game in business. If a customer is satisfied with a level of service, they will become a repeat customer and then, possibly, a loyal one. The goal is to keep that loyal customer happy and enable them to talk about you online. That's not ground-breaking news. But what is new is how new customers are finding you.

It's a fact. Online reviews are impacting virtually every business today. From restaurants and hotels to retail stores and the products on their shelves, to even physicians and lawyers, online reviews have become a strong influence in a consumer's decision to choose your business. Customers now have many options to learn more about your products or services long before they step foot in your store or peruse your website.

The social trust impact of reviews is universal

With over 315 million users, TripAdvisor has long been the authority for online reviews in the hospitality sector. But now sites like Yelp provide reviews of restaurants and service-based companies. According to 2015 site statistics, an average of 26,000 reviews are posted per minute. Amazon, touting over 244 million users, has become the "go to" provider for consumers to purchase practically anything through its unique distribution model and the platform gives consumers the ability to easily review the products they purchased. Providers like Angie's List, with an average of 3 million users, now provide reviews on professional services such as physician providers.

If you want to see more examples of consumer reviews, just Google the product or service you're interested in and add the word "reviews". Here are a few examples:

- TireRack.com for tires
- Avvo.com for lawyers
- CreditKarma.com for credit cards, loans, insurance, banks, etc.
- G2Crowd.com for business software
- RateMyProfessors.com for colleges and universities and their professors
- Vitals.com and Healthgrades.com for medical professionals

More research than ever before

Consumers are spending more time researching companies prior to purchasing goods and services. In a 2015 study by BrightLocal, 85% of consumers said they read up to 10 reviews and 7% of consumers said they read 20+ reviews. This signifies more engagement with review sites, but it may also highlight trust issues.

There is an interesting phenomenon with online reviews. Consumers are listening to the opinions and experiences of total strangers as they evaluate your business. They don't want to be "sold" or "marketed"; but instead want to hear other REAL customers describe their perceptions of your business. This highlights the importance of having at least 10 reviews to satisfy 85% of potential customers. It goes without saying these reviews should not only be positive, but also fresh. If consumers only read the latest reviews, it's crucial to ensure the most recent reviews are positive.

SECRET #2

Customers communicate hidden patterns in their online reviews

What I love – and I'm a journalist – and what I love is finding hidden patters; I love being a data detective."

David McCandless –
Data Journalist and Information Designer

"One of the pleasures of looking at the world through mathematical eyes is that you can see certain patterns that would otherwise be hidden."

Steven Strogatz –Mathematician and Professor

If you are like most of the leaders we speak with, you may be aware that your customers are more actively writing online reviews to express their experiences and are using online reviews to determine if they are going to do business with you or your competitors. However, you might be surprised at how much of an impact these reviews are having. Typically, after we share the first secret of online reviews, leaders say, "But, I read all the reviews. What more can you tell me than I already know?"

The answer is, "A lot!"

Online reviews contain a variety of patterns. Some are relevant across all industries we have researched including hotels and restaurants, doctors and lawyers, even sports arenas or retail stores and the products they sell. Other patterns are specific to the industry. Yet others are unique to the company or product being reviewed. These patterns are hidden to the untrained eye. They only emerge with extensive experience. Often, they are invisible even to the most popular software products on the market that are designed to mine these online reviews.

Balancing the expert and the software

In the fall of 2015, Tony presented a compelling series of case studies at an industry conference showing that most text-mining software products are missing three to five of the fundamental text analysis capabilities that a human can be trained to see and which are essential for deriving valuable insights. This doesn't mean the tools are unnecessary. In their current state they perform a vital role in automating the analysis of themes you know how to detect. They also accelerate the process of monitoring issues that are critical to the organization. And, the software can process vast quantities of data that human analysts would take weeks or months to review. As new patterns are defined by analysts, the existing software is being updated or new software is being invented to automate what, at one time, only human analysts were capable of.

Patterns experts found

Following are some of the most common patterns, not yet detectable by the software packages we've used for analysis. These patterns emerge based on the ratings a customer provides.

Customers who give an "Excellent" rating will typically praise a particular staff member or a particular department for a job well done. You will seldom see an excellent rating that does not include the mention of a staff member or a leader. However, below the excellent rating, it is unlikely that there will be a positive mention of a specific person or even a team as a whole.

Looking down the scale to a "Fair" experience, typically at the midpoint of the ratings, the customer will discuss features of the product or the experience and mention that the benefits of these features were adequate for the price paid. Usually there is a balancing act by the consumer between rating the pros and cons of the features and the benefits or lack of benefits experienced. In other words, customers experience the transaction as a fair deal. But, we have noted that this is also where customers indicate that, while they don't regret their purchase this one time, they would not buy this product or invest in this experience again.

Finally, looking at the reviews with a "Poor" rating, or the lowest score on the scale, customers are likely to express their anger or discontent and may even go so far as to say they were "robbed." These customers may use all capital letters and strongly discourage readers from ever doing business with the company. These are damaging reviews and can leave a powerful, negative impression on the reader.

While these are just a few of the patterns we've identified across industries, we have been able to show clients there is a clear and significant distinction between each rating level. In addition, there is a clear set of patterns for customers who rate above versus below average. Beyond that, we see that customer awareness of issues before they buy may offset some problems, but awareness alone is often not nearly enough to make up for every challenge the customer will experience. These patterns matter because they can be used to focus your continuous improvement efforts or to hone your marketing language and sales scripts.

Patterns reveal consumer mindset

These hidden language patterns are a result of a predictable mindset that each segment of customers has. The language of these written reviews is often a subconscious expression, not thought through consciously and dispassionately, so they reveal details about what the customer believes, what they expected and how they feel about their experience. With expert understanding, the mindset of the customer can be identified and used to help in the response to the individual review as well as in the planning of the tactical, operational and strategic actions the company will take to eliminate the issues for future customers.

PRACTICAL INSIGHTS

TONY BODOH & KAYLA BARRETT

SECRET #3

Employee engagement directly impacts the customer experience

Your employees come first. And if you treat your employees right, guess what? Your customers come back, and that makes your shareholders happy. Start with employees and the rest follows from that."

Herb Kelleher – Co-Founder, Southwest Airlines

"Employees who believe that management is concerned about them as a whole person – not just an employee – are more productive, more satisfied, more fulfilled. Satisfied employees mean satisfied customers, which leads to profitability."

Anne M. Mulcahy –
Former Chairman and CEO, Xerox

Companies that fully understand the impact of research supporting customer loyalty and take appropriate actions have a competitive advantage in the marketplace. Not only do they take intentional measures to create remarkable customer experiences, they also don't stop short of the full picture.

Customer experience depends upon the employee

We know that a key driver behind the customer experience is the employee. Products and services must be superb but your employees impact every interaction customers have with your business. A great deal of focus has been placed on employee satisfaction; however recent research supports that when outstanding customer service occurs, the motivation is much deeper than traditional employee satisfaction levels.

Gallup's 2012 research revealed that as the economy began to rebound in 2009, an engaged workforce was a critical differentiator in earnings per share (EPS). Companies with an average of 9 engaged employees for every actively disengaged employee in 2010-2011 experienced 147% higher EPS compared to competition in the same time period. In contrast, companies with an average of 2 engaged employees for every disengaged employee experienced 2% less EPS than the competition.

It's a fact. Engaged employees provide service that goes beyond standard expectations. And that level of service creates an experience that is so positive that customers feel compelled to tell others. It is a form of reciprocation in action. The experience was so good—worth so much more than they feel they paid—that the customer wants to serve the company. They do this by writing reviews, recommending the company or making referrals. These engagement studies show us that organizations that tap into their greatest sales asset—employees—yield the greatest results. And that is crucial in today's social media environment.

How engaged and disengaged employees differ

To illustrate this concept, consider an example from the hospitality industry. Hotels today are much more than overnight lodging. Incremental revenues drive profitability as guests (customers) purchase dining and other additional amenities.

An engaged employee will likely ask his leader if they can experience some of the hotel's restaurants or amenities so that he can describe these experiences to a guest. He believes in these products or services and wants guests to experience them as well. He will use adjectives that evoke interest in the service (i.e. "pamper yourself in our relaxing escape") and he won't give up at the first objection or rejection.

In contrast, a disengaged employee may not even offer the additional service and if he does, it may likely resemble the typical add-on in the fast food industry, "Do you want fries with that?" If the guest says no, he simply moves on in the transaction. This is a key difference: The engaged employee expands the experience; the disengaged employee closes the transaction.

Employee engagement impacts online reviews

Now, take that same example with your engaged employee and consider how it translates to online reviews. That guest is ten times more likely to share her experience online and will often mention the helpfulness of the employee in the review. The level of employee engagement has a direct impact on the customer experience.

So, let's take a quick test. How well can you answer these questions?

- What do your employees say about your business to their network of friends and colleagues?
- How many of your employees have experienced your business as a customer?
- And finally, how well can your competitor answer these questions?

In today's environment, what does an engaged employee look like?

He or she shows up each day actively seeking ways to make your business better. They are proactive in the aspects of their role—they don't simply identify customer irritants but they create possible solutions. Their awareness skills are heightened—they actively observe customers to identify ways to provide service and offer value to them. They guide interactions with customers versus simply being responsive to them. And finally, they are the reason customers share their 5-star experiences with others.

Paradigm shifts to build an engaged team
So, how do you turn this ship? It requires a paradigm shift in every aspect of the employee life cycle.

A different approach to talent selection occurs. Proven service mindsets are vetted during the interview process and the business won't "settle" to the pressure of filling an empty slot.

A different approach to operations also emerges. Product knowledge and experience—both depth and breadth— becomes a focus in training and development. Your leaders coach employees by targeting communication and comprehensive selling and service skills.

And finally, a different approach to rewards occurs. For example, reward systems shift to focus on developing relationships with the customer that naturally grow sales and generate revenue versus solely on traditional performance metrics.

These integrated strategies will positively impact your employee engagement, which in turn creates remarkable customer experiences. And guess what? Those customers feel compelled to tell others about your business…and they do. And, when that occurs, revenue growth is a natural outcome. It's the psychology of smart and successful businesses.

PRACTICAL INSIGHTS

THE COMPLETE EXPERIENCE

SECRET #4

**Focus on solving the right problem, not reacting
to a poor review**

Discipline is the bridge between goals and accomplishment."

Jim Rohn – Entreprenuer and Motivational Speaker

*"Our age knows nothing but reaction, and leaps from one
extreme to another."*

Reinhold Niebuhr – Theologian and Ethicist

There is a powerful outcome for companies who become disciplined about understanding the depth and themes discovered in customer online reviews. Armed with a data-driven diagnosis, impactful solutions can be created that accurately address real-time customer issues versus the sporadic approach most companies are left with as they attempt to address the myriad of negative online reviews received.

Our ongoing online reviews research reveals three common themes for the types of action that typically emerge from customer comments—strategic, operational, and tactical:

Types of strategic decisions
Decisions made and actions taken by senior leaders that define the intended customer experience are strategic.

Examples include:
- A hotel may ensure that each front desk agent dines at the property's restaurants so they can use enticing and descriptive language to guests during the check-in process.

- A retail shop may conduct weekly or monthly customer experience meetings to review online reviews, then identify emerging trends and possible action strategies that create long-term results.

- A restaurant may delay capital improvements to its parking infrastructure because customer feedback prioritizes an improvement to restroom facilities first.

Types of operational decisions

Decisions made and actions taken by mid-level leaders that affect the service level provided to customers are of an operational nature.

Examples include:

- A retailer may change employee schedules to ensure more service levels are available to match the production schedules of nearby entertainment venues.

- A restaurant may conduct a focus group to gather the feedback on the restaurant's customer experience. A free meal is served during the focus group where questions are asked to discover the top three service strengths and top three service issues.

- An electric company may partner each customer service representative with a lineman or meter reader (and vice versa) so each can better understand a "day in the life" of each other's roles and how those impact the customer experience.

Types of tactical decisions

Decisions made and actions taken by frontline employees that affect the customer's experience in the moment are tactical.

Examples include:

- A restaurant employee may experiment using her own positive adjectives to describe various menu options to customers.

- A bank employee may time herself to ensure customers are greeted within 30 seconds of entering the bank lobby.

- A help desk employee may include a brief feedback question to internal customers to gather specific feedback on ways he can improve the phone experience.

Why this matters
Without a process for prioritizing solution strategies, most companies fall into the trap of responding to poor reviews with a one-off approach. The complaint is often funneled to the appropriate department; the issue is corrected and a follow-up message is sent to the customer. In theory, this sounds like a "responsive" company; however, when a broader perspective is taken, like we suggest above, companies can assess where the right focus should be placed that will create the greatest impact to: 1) common problem themes plaguing the company; and, 2) the company's online ranking.

Another benefit of this intentional focus is the opportunity to become more efficient in improvement efforts. Too often companies try to pursue numerous efforts simultaneously which actually decreases the overall effectiveness of any one initiative. In reality, there is likely a long list of issues in your business that need attention. However, in the spirit of "working smarter, not harder," prioritized efforts actually create momentum opportunities for your business. Consider the potential if every department in your company was focused on improving one service behavior. Two benefits occur: 1) every employee is focused and unified in the same direction; and, 2) customers experience a visible difference in the service they receive.

A prioritized approach to the issues that matter create positive results for all involved: customers win because they see positive changes in the business (they feel heard); employees win because they see how their efforts are making a difference (they feel engaged); and the business wins because increased sales will follow (greater revenue occurs).

THE COMPLETE EXPERIENCE

PRACTICAL INSIGHTS

TONY BODOH & KAYLA BARRETT

.

SECRET #5

Everyone wins when the vision is clear

"Every creator painfully experiences the chasm between his inner vision and its ultimate expression."

Isaac Bashevis Singer – Nobel Prize in Literature

"It takes someone with a vision of the possibilities to attain new levels of experience. Someone with the courage to live his dreams."

Les Brown – Author and Motivational Speaker

Over the last ten years, we've consulted with some of the top, award-winning, customer experience leading companies. One thing that is consistent is they have a vague notion of what they want their ideal customer experience to be. These companies have become the leaders in their industry by focusing on: 1) investing in customer features and benefits; 2) working harder than they needed; and, 3) creating cultures of heroes where the effort of individual employees, not repeatable processes and procedures, is really the cause of their success.

Why you need a customer experience vision

The dark side to this reality is that these companies cannot sustain their level of success. In fact, they often reach out to us after they have fallen from their leadership position in the industry or when they see a competitor quickly closing the gap that they expected would always be there. With the loss of that differentiation as the clear leader, their market share drops, their best customers start to leave and profitability declines.

One of the key reasons this happens is because the company had no clearly defined vision of what they would love their ideal customer experience to be. Sure, there may be a corporate mission and they may say they want to be "the provider of choice" but what does that really mean to the customer? What does that mean to the employee in the call center on the phone with an angry customer? What does that mean to the product manager who is trying to design the next new innovation?

The fact is, most companies consider the work of visioning their ideal customer experience silly at best or a waste of resources at worst. However, when pressed for an explanation of how they will know that they have achieved what they set out to achieve, the most common answer is "Our customers will give us 10s."

What is a ten?

To a single mom who is working, a ten may be completely different than to the mom who is married and volunteers at the PTA. And, over time what customers expect changes so what it takes to achieve the ten will also change.

Without a clear description of the ideal experience for each key customer segment, the products and services your company provides will never really address the needs, wants and desires of any customer in an effective manner for an extended period of time. Instead, your products and services will be an average of the expectations of all customers and they will lack anything that really distinguishes them in the marketplace.

Winners act to realize their clear vision
The competitor who will win is the one who is willing to customize their product or service for a specific customer segment. This means the company truly understands the emotions of their customer before a purchase; where the company wants the customer to move emotionally during the engagement; and where the customer expects to be as a result of using the product or service. This is expected in today's data-rich customer environment.

It is vitally important for the company to set aside all of their market research and internal data for a while and go within. They need to start by asking themselves, "What would we love to hear (insert key customer segment) saying about our company, products and services to their best friend?"

This exercise requires some soul searching and it requires imagination. But more than that, it requires the willingness to turn off the analytical mind for a while because the purpose of this exercise is to tune into the emotions of the customer. It is not the time or the place to figure out how you will achieve this desired state. That comes later, after you have made a committed decision to really deliver the ideal customer experience to this segment of customers.

PRACTICAL INSIGHTS

TONY BODOH & KAYLA BARRETT

FROM SECRETS TO SOLUTIONS

A game plan to begin your own success story

"Inspiration without action is merely entertainment."

Mary Morrissey – Author and Executive Coach

"Just do it."

Nike's Slogan

Our intent in writing this book was to give you a deeper understanding of the impact that online reviews have on your business today and the influence they will inevitably have tomorrow. However, we did not think it was good enough to only reveal some of the secrets we have discovered in our ten years of work in this field. We want you to have a plan of action. Below, we outline key steps that you can and should take immediately to make progress in improving your customers' experiences and as a result, their online reviews.

15 Steps for defining the vision of your ideal customer experience

Step 1
Answer the question: "What would we love to hear our customers saying about our company, products or services to their best friends?"

Step 2
Use as many descriptive words as possible to provide clarity to the ideal experience.

Step 3
Rewrite any sections of the vision where you use internal acronyms, product features or other phrases that are not really the language of a customer.

Step 4
Ask your team to review and comment on the vision: Is it clear, concise, compelling, complete and creative?

Step 5
Compare and contrast your customers' online reviews to your new vision.

Step 6
Print out some online reviews from the past month.

Step 7
Read each review and mark descriptive words that align with your vision with a green highlighter and use a red highlighter to mark words that are counter to your vision.

Step 8
Circulate these reviews and ask your team for ideas on why these things may be happening.

Step 9
Explore every hypothesis with a root cause analysis to ensure that it is real and not just an opinion.

Step 10
Determine your investment priority to close the gap between the reviews and your vision. Remember to consider strategic, operational and tactical investments.

Step 11
List the areas of customer concerns that will move your lowest scores up first. Then proceed up your ratings to the next level. Finally, list those areas that will move up the above average scores.

Step 12
Identify what specific actions to take to solve the top problems on the list.

Step 13
Budget and create a project plan with timelines to solve these problems.

Step 14
Create an accountability program that is inspiring, not
overbearing.

Step 15
Act now!

In the next section you will read about some of the
companies who have followed our recommendations and
the results they achieved. We know that with the right
commitment to action and the alignment of the
organization from the top to customer-facing employees,
your company can succeed in improving your customers'
experiences and their reviews.

THE COMPLETE EXPERIENCE

PRACTICAL INSIGHTS

TONY BODOH & KAYLA BARRETT

SUCCESS STORIES

Inspiration from those who have learned these secrets

"The price of success is hard work, dedication to the job at hand, and the determination that whether we win or we lose, we have applied the best of ourselves to the task at hand."

Vince Lombardi – Head Coach Green Bay Packers

"The starting point of all achievement is desire."

Napoleon Hill –
Author and Father of Personal Development

The previous pages have given you a behind-the-scenes look at the many facets of online customers reviews. In today's marketplace, they matter like never before. As we conclude, read how these truths have helped real businesses. We have used hotel companies in these examples to demonstrate the impact this approach can have on a specific industry.

Increase Revenue and Conversion Rates

A resort wanted to improve its conversion rates on upsells offered while checking in. We analyzed the current processes and language used by the staff as well as guest feedback and behaviors. We discovered some hidden triggers in the check-in experience that caused guests to decline the invitation to upgrade their room. As a result, we developed a custom training program for all reservation agents and front desk employees. The tailored education focused on a behavioral sales model linked to the identified guest triggers. The week following the training, the teams generated 400% more room upgrades than in any previous week.

Improve Customer Retention and Reduce Customer Churn

Meeting planners were threatening to pull tens of thousands of guest room nights from one of the largest hotels in the U.S. because of service issues. We partnered with the hotel to review guest feedback. We discovered a key phrase in the script used by the reservations staff which set improper expectations for the guests. Three weeks after updating the script and equipping the team with a new service response, the hotel doubled their satisfaction scores and the meeting planners withdrew their threats. A redefined focus on the employee/guest equation established a new foundation of behavior for each guest-facing employee. Now the hotel is highly recommended in the meeting planner community as "the place to go."

Improve Cost per Acquisition
A hotel company that relied on online reviews and recommendations for a large portion of its sales was only receiving a combined 11% "Good" and "Excellent" ratings on TripAdvisor.com. We analyzed the feedback guests provided and recommended the hotel make a significant investment in an area that had been neglected previously. This process revealed a new way for the hotel to understand and utilize its TripAdvisor data. The hotel now has a combined 76% "Good" and "Excellent" rating on TripAdvisor.com and the hotel soared to where it now outranks 4-star, major-brand hotels in its market. The hotel's occupancy rates increased while the cost per acquisition dropped because new guests trusted the positive reviews of previous guests.

Where to Invest in Capital Improvements
The flagship property of a hotel brand was planning a $300 million capital improvement project. Just before approving the project, the COO of the brand asked us to assess the need and potential impact of the renovation. Based on guest feedback and behaviors, we found that the investment would not net the return that the pro forma model suggested. The company halted the project and invested in a more promising project.

Create an Advantage in Negotiations with Vendors
A hotel ownership group was in negotiations with their outsourced valet provider. The president of the group asked if we could provide data-driven support for their position to reduce costs or determine if they should seek a new provider. We reviewed guest feedback and found that the president's intuition was on point. The valet was a cause of much negative feedback from guests and was actually diminishing the brand's reputation and value. As a

result, the negotiations ended in favor of the hotel ownership group. They saved money and the valet service improved due to new training that was implemented.

FIND YOUR OWN SECRETS AND SURPRISES

★ ★ ★ ★ ★

Imagine the possibilities…

"I have no special talent. I am only passionately curious."

Albert Einstein– Nobel Prize in Physics

"Without imagination we can go nowhere. And imagination is not restricted to the arts. Every scientist I have met who has been a success has had to imagine."

Rita Dove – Poet and Author

Imagine what could happen with your business if you learned the secret language of its online reviews.

What if?
What if you really learned what your customers think as they write a review of their experience with you, your employees and business?

And better yet, just imagine what is in store when you have not just customers, but loyal customers.

Start now.
The possibilities are endless. Start your journey now. Go back to the section "From Secrets to Solutions" and start defining your ideal customer experience.

Focus on taking just one step at a time. You don't need to do it all at once. And, it doesn't need to be perfect. Taking consistent small steps in the right direction is what will make the difference in your company over time.

PRACTICAL INSIGHTS

THE COMPLETE EXPERIENCE

SOURCES

2015 Talent Trends by LinkedIn Talent Solutions

Amazon Statistics
https://www.statista.com/topics/846/amazon/

Angie's List Statistics
http://support.business.angieslist.com/app/answers/detail/a_id/199/~/how-many-members-does-angies-list-have%3F

Consumers Trust Online Reviews
http://searchengineland.com/88-consumers-trust-online-reviews-much-personal-recommendations-195803

Employee Engagement Drives Growth
http://www.gallup.com/businessjournal/163130/employee-engagement-drives-growth.aspx

Online Reviews Impact Small Business
http://www.inc.com/michael-fertik/online-reviews-make-big-difference-small-business.html

TripAdvisor Statistics
http://www.telegraph.co.uk/travel/travelnews/11242887/TripAdvisor-in-numbers.html

Yelp Statistics
http://expandedramblings.com/index.php/yelp-statistics/3/

ABOUT THE AUTHORS

Kayla Barrett

Light bulbs are one of Kayla's favorite things. More specifically, light bulbs coming on in people's heads. Kayla is a thinker and practitioner in today's marketplace. She helps organizations drive growth by creating and sustaining their competitive advantage. Through strategies that develop the critical talent, skills and capabilities, employee and customer engagement grow resulting in bottom-line results. Her industry experience spans 20+ years in both the corporate sector and non-profit world where she has worn hats such as Director of Organizational Strategy, Director of Human Resources and Director of Staff Development.

Kayla's experience allows her to walk alongside your team to identify your people development needs then helps you discover a hands-on approach that advances your organization's vision and profitability. She is president of Organization Impact, LLC and a member of the Society of Human Resources Management, American Society of Training and Development, Southeast Business Forum, and Phi Kappa Phi Honor Society. Kayla holds a BS and MS in Organizational Communication from Murray State University. She is a certified DiSC facilitator and the author of "Leadership Shorts: Practical Tips When You Are at Wit's End". Organization Impact is a member of the Better Business Bureau.

Tony Bodoh

Tony learned at an early age the power of listening and letting people know they've been heard. He started a lawncare business at 11 years old. While his friends had one or two lawns to cut, Tony kept busy all summer with 16 clients.

Tony is the founder or co-founder of five companies ranging from customer experience consulting to small business training to television. He easily navigates the international stage speaking at both personal growth seminars as well as the uber-nerdy technology conferences. Tony writes business blogs, personal growth essays and children's stories. While he now coaches executives, he taught high school for one year and in the Business Department of Aquinas College in Nashville, Tennessee for seven years.

As a passionate believer in the power and possibility that is contained in each moment of human experience to alter the course of history, Tony financially supports the building of sustainable villages in Africa and Haiti. He donates his time at his daughters' school and serves as the mental performance coach for the Nashville Irish Step Dancers.

Tony resides in Nashville with his wife Julie who is an executive chef and his two daughters who are award-winning Irish Step Dancers and earned two Guinness Book of World Records before they were 10 years old.

CONNECT WITH THE AUTHORS

Connect with Kayla
CEO, Organization Impact, LLC
Email: kayla@organizationimpact.com
Twitter: @kaylabarrett2
LinkedIn: Kayla Barrett
FaceBook: Organization Impact
Blog/Podcast: www.organizationimpact.com

Connect with Tony
CEO, Tony Bodoh International LLC
Email: Tony@TonyBodoh.com
Twitter: @TonyBodoh
LinkedIn: Tony Bodoh
Blog: www.TonyBodoh.com

Learn more at
www.TheCompleteExperience.com

www.ingramcontent.com/pod-product-compliance
Lightning Source LLC
Chambersburg PA
CBHW050522210326
41520CB00012B/2401